# Valley of the Cranes

## EXPLORING COLORADO'S SAN LUIS VALLEY

PHOTOGRAPHS BY

WENDY SHATTIL and
ROBERT ROZINSKI

ESSAY BY

VIRGINIA McCONNELL SIMMONS

ROBERTS RINEHART, INC. PUBLISHERS

Front Cover

SANDHILLS IN STEAM OF NIGHT ROOST The floor of the San Luis Valley provides a seasonal home for migrating sandhill cranes. Water from flowing artesian wells creates a comparatively warm environment for a roost when temperatures at night can otherwise dip to -25 degrees.

Back Cover

STRING OF CANADA GEESE AGAINST SANGRES The Sangre de Cristos, one of two mountain ranges ringing the San Luis Valley, provide the backdrop for a string of Canada geese flying to a feeding ground at sunrise.



Published by Roberts Rinehart, Inc. Publishers

Post Office Box 666, Niwot, Colorado 80544

International Standard Book Numbers 0-911797-41-6 (cloth) and 0-911797-49-1 (paper)

Library of Congress Catalog Card Number 88-61286

Printed in the United States of America

Designed by Ann W. Douden

Typesetting by Lyn Chaffee/Archetype

Production by J. Keith Abernathy

## Contents

Acknowledgments • The publisher would like to acknowledge the grateful assistance of the following individuals and organizations, without whose support *Valley of the Cranes* would not have been possible: Adams State College; Alamosa Chamber of Commerce; Alamosa Chamber Development Corporation; Alamosa County Board of Commissioners; Bank of Monte Vista; Best Western Movie Manor Restaurant and Motel; the City of Alamosa; Colorado Insurance Associates; Karen and Max Deacon; First National Bank of Alamosa; Ignacio "Nacho" Martinez; Monte Vista Chamber of Commerce; San Luis Valley Board of Realtors; San Luis Valley Economic Development Council; San Luis Valley Federal Savings and Loan; San Luis Valley Potato Administrative Committee; Staley Manufacturing; Amy and Byron Uhrich; Valley-6 Promotional Council; Vendola Plumbing; and Wright Brothers, Inc.

Our gratitude goes to Virginia Simmons, Amy Uhrich, and Rick Rinehart for making this project viable and uncompromising. We also appreciate the special help extended by many residents of the San Luis Valley, particularly Melvin Nail, Donna Kingery, Bert Widhalm, Errol Ryland, and Whitney Strong. *Wendy Shattil and Robert Rozinski*

I wish to thank Melvin T. Nail, D. H. McFadden, Jr., Dorothy McFadden, and Amy Uhrich for reading the first draft of the manuscript and offering suggestions for the final text. *Virginia McConnell Simmons*

Foreword • *Valley of the Cranes: Exploring Colorado's San Luis Valley* represents a cooperative effort on the part of a number of people who wished to draw attention to and pay tribute to one of our state's most scenic and historic regions. Photographers Wendy Shattil and Bob Rozinski initiated this project to record the Valley's many wonderful natural features. Their dedication has resulted in numerous images that have won national and international acclaim. Virginia McConnell Simmons, well-known Colorado author, has written a text that describes the poetry of this land in prose. The book is being published with the enthusiastic encouragement of Frederick R. Rinehart, president of Roberts Rinehart, Inc. Publishers of Boulder, Colorado. Amy Uhrich of Monte Vista arranged for advances to the author and photographers through grants from twenty-one individuals and organizations in the San Luis Valley. Their sponsorship has made them key participants in a literary and artistic project about the natural riches of the area. The result of this collaboration is *Valley of the Cranes.* In the pages to follow, the photographers and author will share with you their vision of Great Sand Dunes National Monument, Wheeler Geologic Area, the Monte Vista National Wildlife Refuge, and many other special places. The story that is told in this book is vivid and true and carries with it a love for an extraordinary place in Colorado. *Roy Romer, Governor*

Introduction • Nearing the end of summer and our imminent deadline to complete photography for this book, we found ourselves waiting for sunset at the Pinnacles in Saguache Park. We stopped simultaneously in mid-conversation, hearing a sound at once familiar, yet curiously out of place. It took but a moment for the realization to hit us: the sandhill cranes were returning to the San Luis Valley. Just then the first string of migrating birds glided over us in their descent to the Valley floor. Their arrival seemed to us the perfect way to conclude our work on this book, and solidified the inspiration for its title, *Valley of the Cranes.*

"Bigger than Connecticut," our playful working title until that spirited moment in Saguache Park, only begins to describe the San Luis Valley's size. That's impressive, but the true allure lies in the people, the astounding diversity of terrain, and an elusive feeling that this is simply a very special place—a quality so strong humans have been drawn to the Valley for the past 12,000 years.

In our over 20,000 miles of driving and photographing the Valley, we found places so unique we were almost reluctant to share them. But we have. If our work encourages you to explore and experience the Valley of the Cranes then you, too, may fall under its spell and return again and again.

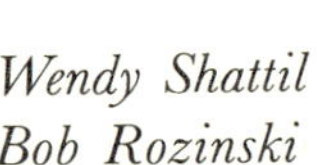

*Wendy Shattil*
*Bob Rozinski*

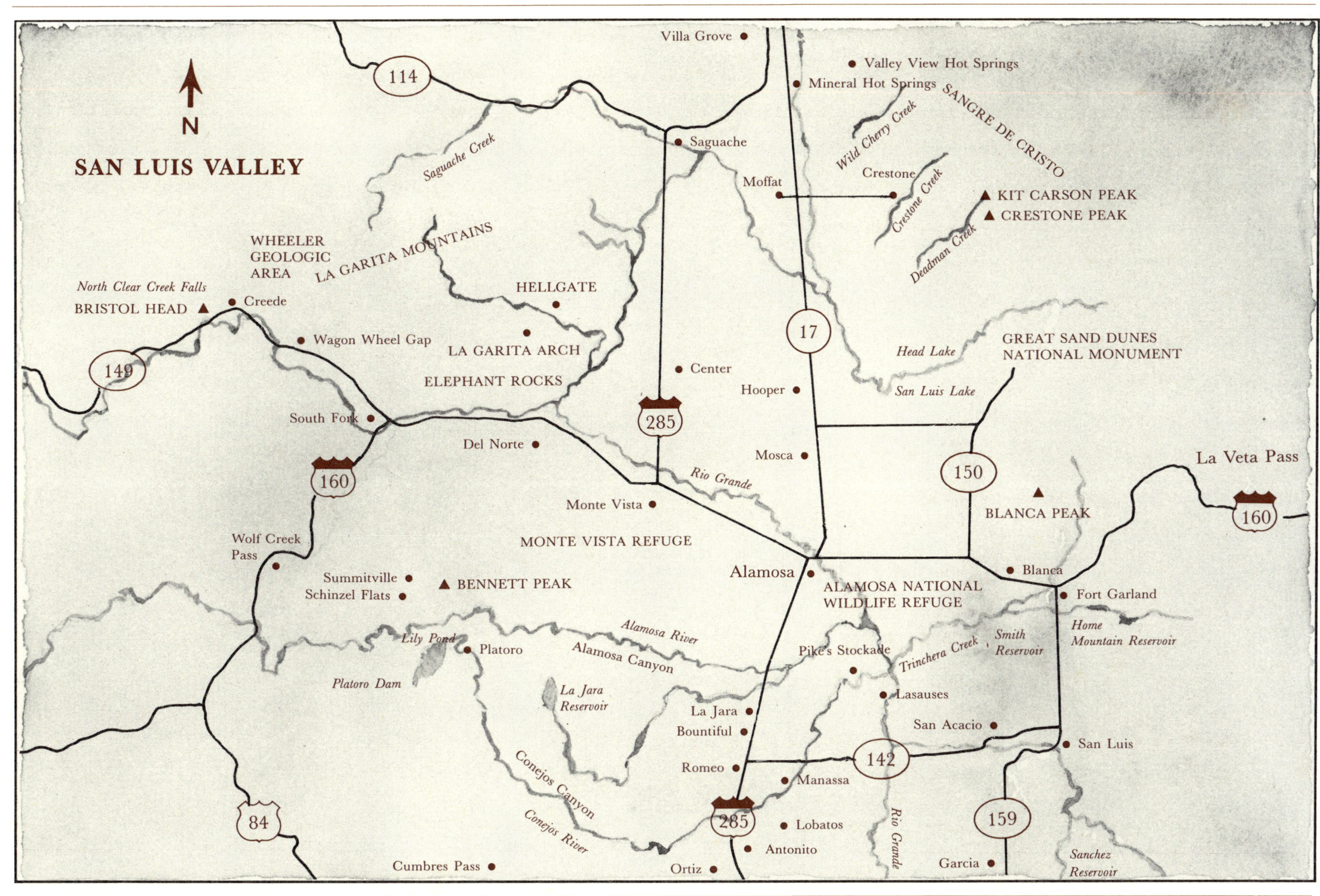
N
SAN LUIS VALLEY
Villa Grove
114
Valley View Hot Springs
Mineral Hot Springs
SANGRE DE CRISTO
Saguache
Saguache Creek
Wild Cherry Creek
Moffat
Crestone
Crestone Creek
KIT CARSON PEAK
CRESTONE PEAK
Deadman Creek
WHEELER GEOLOGIC AREA
LA GARITA MOUNTAINS
North Clear Creek Falls
BRISTOL HEAD
Creede
HELLGATE
Wagon Wheel Gap
LA GARITA ARCH
17
Head Lake
GREAT SAND DUNES NATIONAL MONUMENT
149
ELEPHANT ROCKS
Center
Hooper
San Luis Lake
285
South Fork
Del Norte
Mosca
160
Rio Grande
150
La Veta Pass
Monte Vista
BLANCA PEAK
160
Wolf Creek Pass
MONTE VISTA REFUGE
Alamosa
Blanca
Summitville
Schinzel Flats
BENNETT PEAK
ALAMOSA NATIONAL WILDLIFE REFUGE
Fort Garland
Home Mountain Reservoir
Alamosa River
Lily Pond
Platoro
Alamosa Canyon
Pike's Stockade
Trinchera Creek
Smith Reservoir
Platoro Dam
La Jara Reservoir
Lasauses
La Jara
Bountiful
San Acacio
San Luis
Romeo
142
Manassa
Conejos Canyon
Conejos River
Rio Grande
84
285
Lobatos
159
Antonito
Sanchez Reservoir
Cumbres Pass
Ortiz
Garcia

Between two masses of mountains in south-central Colorado lies the San Luis Valley. It is impossible to visualize this high intermontane basin without including the peaks that provide a physical frame for the Valley and play an integral role in its life. Indeed, the ongoing creation and shaping of the ranges have been responsible for the formation of the Valley itself.

Water and stone, snow and wind continue to slip and tumble thousands of feet down to the Valley floor, millions of years after volcanic eruptions heralded the birth of the San Juan Mountains and after the Sangre de Cristo Range was thrust upward. Down the slopes, streams carry tons of alluvium every year to fan out as aprons of gravel and sand along the foothills and onto the Valley's bed, like the residue of artists molding and carving the mountains above.

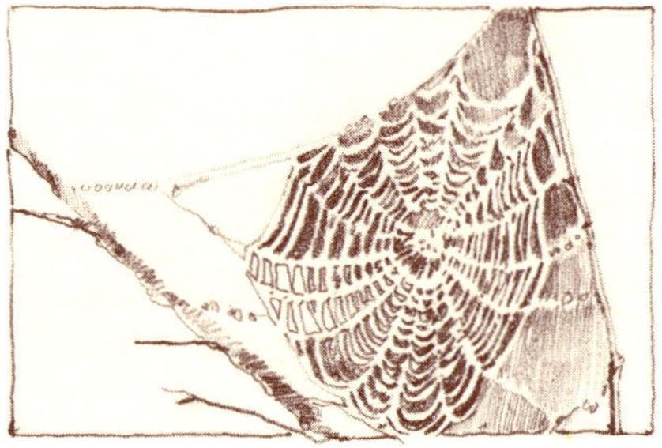

Beneath this deposit lies a deep aquifer of water that has cascaded down to the Valley and seeped through the strata. Also, the Rio Grande, threading a wide path through the Valley, gathers unto itself many flowing streams and drains them southward, for here in the high summits ringing the Valley the Rio Grande's long journey to the Gulf of Mexico begins. These sources of water profoundly affect life in the arid Valley.

Not only is the region's agricultural economy dependent on this life-giving water, but also wildlife is drawn to streams and ponds. Each spring and fall clouds of migratory birds follow the Rio Grande along one of the major flyways of the North American continent. Among these birds are the cranes.

Such cyclic patterns have a regularity to them that is predictable, or nearly so, and we humans tend to find security in recognizing nature's repetitiousness and continuity. In so doing, we overlook the slow but revolutionary changes that created this wondrous place by means of geologic uplift and fiery volcanoes, faulting and glaciers. We take for granted today's shape of the land and the uses to which we put it. We share rangelands and farmlands with antelope and coyotes, deer and jackrabbits matter-of-factly. We forget the ancient mammoths and extinct species of buffalo which grazed here in a long-gone age, a time when the climate was more moist and vegetation was different. We forget to wonder what changes lie ahead.

With our limited perspective, we see change only as the stubborn progression of seasons. Perhaps it is understandable that these magical transitions represent change for most of us, as birth and death, growth and decay occur from the Valley's cactus-studded floor to alpine tundra. With fields of yellow dandelions, blue iris, and magenta fireweed exclaiming the joy of new life, no one remembers the wolves, the otters, the cutthroat trout, the grizzly bears that do not return. Armadas of ducklings assure us each summer that neither nature's caprice nor man's meddling have destroyed this paradise yet. And, after all, the cranes keep to their coming and going.

Only in autumn, when winter waits in the wings, when the golden glory of shimmering aspens brings a lump to the throat, do we acknowledge that change can be loss, perhaps permanent. Then we remember to mumble a half-spoken prayer that somehow the streams, the flowers, the wildlife, the mysterious mountains, and we will be together another season. And so it is that we gratefully relish the faint aroma of ponderosa pines on a sun-warmed hillside at the close of a rock-splitting, cold winter.

The San Luis Valley is a gentle land, and it is a harsh land. It is a big land of astonishing contrast. It is the sort of place a person may leave, but, just as it dominates the life within it, it holds firmly the memories of those who attempt to go. The beauty and the sternness, the magic and the mystery cling.

Human imagination compresses events such as the creation of a mountain range into a relatively brief, sudden occurrence, but the outbursts of volcanoes and fracturing of the earth's crust which gave birth to the San Juan Mountains persisted for millions of years. Grinding and polishing still continue, as if to perfect their form, and there is much room for artistic dabbling by nature in this bulky, meandering range, where many centers of volcanic activity at different periods of time resulted in several units of mountains.

Today, however, this great, sprawling range on the west side of the San Luis Valley is a slumbering giant. Especially in winter, when the Continental Divide is wrapped in a blanket of snow, the mountains sleep. It is a sleep broken only by a tossing of the wind or by a shudder of slipping snow. It is a long winter's hibernation that few humans dare disturb.

Travelers with a fair share of caution make their way across Spring Creek Pass to Lake City, across Cumbres–La Manga Pass to New Mexico's Chama Valley, and across notorious Wolf Creek Pass to Pagosa Springs and Durango. Although some of these journeys are undertaken by necessity and with trepidation, others constitute opportunities to enjoy winter sports. Snowmobiling and skiing, either cross-country or downhill, lure many to the high country. Wolf Creek, one of Colorado's veteran ski areas, boasts some of the deepest powder in the nation.

Not aware of the appeal of winter sports, Indians of long ago avoided the San Juans in winter for the most part. Game trails which they followed in summer and fall were forsaken. If travel was necessitated, they resorted to Cochetopa, a relatively low pass northwest of today's Saguache, or traveled along the Chama River, thereby circumventing the mountains.

Spanish soldiers and explorers understood the merit of avoiding the San Juans in winter. So did French Canadian and American trappers, who came down with their beaver pelts by December. United States military expeditions went north, south, or east, but not west from the San Luis Valley in winter. Only John Charles Fremont, leading an expedition to locate a year-round route for a railroad, attempted a crossing of the range in the winter of 1848–49. Before the survivors staggered out of the mountains, all of their 120 mules had starved or frozen to death and 10 men had died, some eaten afterwards by their desperate companions.

In their own good time, the San Juans awaken, stirring faintly on a sunny knoll somewhere along the foothills, throwing off a blanket of snow in a crashing avalanche from a shoulder, nestling back for another forty winks under a late spring snowfall. Gradually game trails packed by the hooves of hundreds of deer, elk, and bighorns become dark paths, crisscrossing fields of lingering snow. Gradually, too, roads become muddy lanes, reaching farther and farther up into the mountains, where swollen streams still interrupt the access of jeeps and hikers, impatient to reclaim the high country. Would-be fishermen fret beside swollen torrents, while down on the Rio Grande rafters and kayakers whoop it up on white water.

If there is a season called spring in the high San Juans, few people see it. It often is summer before the last snowbanks have retreated from the road to Stony Pass. By then many wildflowers have bloomed on exposed slopes. Glacier lilies and marsh marigolds may be replaced already by mats of phlox, king's crown, and gentian. Along the roads up through the forests, columbine and paintbrush will be blooming. And if it rains, inky-cap mushrooms may be ready to spring up beside a puddled road. Rapidly catkins on aspen trees fall, and groves turn deep emerald with leaves that are scarcely full-size before, somewhere on a shaded mountainside, a spray of yellow foliage startles the eye. Summer in the mountains is a race with the southward-moving sun, with plants and animals busily attempting to complete their cycles of reproduction and maturation before snow falls.

Still, miraculously, there are a few warm, languid weeks when hummingbirds flit among the flowers on San Luis Pass and a golden marmot suns himself on a rock above Kite Lake. Alpine brooks chatter among themselves. Boats drift silently across Rio Grande Reservoir, and down toward Wagon Wheel Gap a fly fisherman wades the riverbed. A solitary hiker squints into the sun and chooses his route up the Pyramid. The days slip past, quickly and smoothly, like sand sifting through a child's fingers, and then it is gone.

During these benign weeks, pastures, including one where Fremont met disaster in winter snow, are the grazing grounds of livestock. As drifts melt, flocks of sheep and herds of cattle are trailed into the hills, higher and higher. In these remote ranges, herders often have been the first to find and to gossip about landmarks, such as Fremont's camps.

Sharing the grassy meadows with the livestock are coyotes or perhaps an occasional black bear, and guarding flocks from these marauders is as much excitement as a herder may know all summer. A tent beside a lonely trail, the herder making his rounds on horseback, a dog barking at a stray, the tinkle of a sheep's bell near timberline—these are part of the high country's tranquility. Today an isolated herder, listening to Juarez on his portable radio in a mountain meadow, is part of our wilderness.

Snow may dust the peaks lightly in August, and the first significant storm may strike as early as Labor Day. When the blanket falls high in the peaks in autumn, it merely drives the game down and makes hunters happy. Hunting in the San Juans can be the fulfillment of dreams savored for weeks. Cabins are filled with hunters. Horse trailers and house trailers rattle through the forests to camps, the locations of which are privileged secrets. Down the highways roll pickup trucks, their beds covered with canvas from which bucks' antlers protrude.

Occasionally the dream turns sour if it snows hard and low. When it does, sheriffs and rescue teams have their hands full. Occasionally, too, there is an individual nightmare, as a hunter discovered after he had struggled desperately, but illegally, for his life with a grizzly bear, an endangered bear, quite possibly the only grizzly bear in the entire San Juan Mountain range in the last thirty years. In the mountains, you take your chances.

So rare as to have been believed to be extinct in this region, grizzly bears once roamed far onto the plains of Colorado, but, because of their pugnacious traits, they were killed by early settlers and driven into secluded locations where they could elude hunters. Whether any other grizzlies still exist in the San Juans seems doubtful, as the age of the one killed in the 1980s suggests it was a surviving cub of bears taken three decades earlier.

The San Juan Mountains contain vast amounts of land that fit the mental image, if not the legislated status, of wilderness —isolated, uncompromising, and uncompromised. Not only can wildlife hide out successfully there, but scenery that would draw throngs of spectators elsewhere can be well-kept secrets, too.

One such place is Wheeler Geologic Area, a relatively small, out-of-the-way corner that has survived intact chiefly because it is too remote to be overwhelmed by visitors. Only a few miles across country from Creede, this sixty-acre cluster of rock formations was first reported by sheepherders around the turn of the century. Until then, the weird scene of eroded volcanic tuff had been hidden by surrounding peaks. Not until 1908 did the supervisor of the new Rio Grande National Forest and a hotel operator from Wagon Wheel Gap investigate rumors about the site. A long, difficult horseback ride brought them to the location, 11,500 feet above sea level, with its colorful vista of "spires and domes, castles and cathedrals, mosques and temples," as the pair ecstatically described the formations. Within a year, energetic promoters had obtained a presidential proclamation establishing Wheeler National Monument. The name honored the leader of a government survey which had been in the San Juans without discovering these formations.

Thankfully, postcards never were printed to publicize the "Bee Hives," "Phantom Ship," "Ghosts," and "Lost Souls" that enthusiasts perceived in the group of rocks. Proclamation or not, the monument was too remote for visitors to reach, and it reverted to the national forest's jurisdiction in 1950. For the past generation, Wheeler has been a prime example of contention between people who advocate recreational use of wild places and people who support environmentalist positions. Special-use designation and augmented acreage have given Wheeler Geologic Area a degree of official protection during this period, but conservationists would prefer that the site become part of nearby La Garita Wilderness Area.

Meanwhile, difficult access on trails used by horses, hikers, or jeeps serves as a buffer.

To date, three segments of land in the San Juans have been protected by legislation rather beyond their *ipso facto* circumstances of isolation, though. These are La Garita Wilderness Area, the first to be set aside, followed by Weminuche and South Conejos wildernesses.

Regardless of remoteness, it seems remarkable that crannies like Wheeler were virtually unknown for so long, because prospectors were picking and probing the San Juans assiduously soon after the Pikes Peak Gold Rush began and throughout the rest of the late 1800s. During the short summers, fortune-seekers scrambled into the mountains, panning and sluicing creeks and scratching at seams as snowbanks receded. Beginning in the 1870s and continuing for more than a half century, mines produced silver and gold, lead and zinc, copper and iron.

The first wave of big strikes occurred across the Continental Divide in the vicinity of Silverton, on the heels of departing

Indians who had lost their claim to the region. To haul equipment to the mines and to bring ore out, wagon roads were hacked over the mountain passes. Stagecoaches clattered along the Rio Grande through Wagon Wheel Gap toward Stony Pass and Lake City during the all-too-short, snow-free season. Disappointed prospectors straggled back over the range, and the name Wagon Wheel Gap is said to allude to a broken wheel discarded by one of the first of these parties.

Taking another look east of the Divide, a few prospectors were rewarded by discoveries in the San Juans surrounding the San Luis Valley. The first good producers opened in the 1870s at Summitville, and Del Norte quickly became a bustling supply point for this camp high in the mountains. Farther south, other mines followed in the areas around Jasper, Stunner, and Platoro. These mines in Alamosa Canyon and Conejos Canyon soon were eclipsed, though, by exciting discoveries around Bonanza in the Cochetopa Hills. Several boom towns sprang up around these mines in the north end of the San Luis Valley, and, although most were closed down by the 1930s, some like the Rawley have been worked off and on for more than a century. Along with precious minerals, the area also produced copper and, with it, some fine turquoise, while across the Valley the mountains were yielding economically important quantities of iron and occasional discoveries of gold.

Nothing in this diversity of mining activity quite prepared the Valley for Creede. While other areas opened and closed, prospectors had continued to search the San Juans, along the Rio Grande and its tributaries. Eventually they found what they had been looking for—pay dirt. Holy Moses was the name of the first mine, and that exclamation probably was one of the milder phrases shouted as the San Juans finally revealed their true riches. Names of towns came and went—Jimtown, Bachelor, Spar City, Sky City. One name—Creede—became a legend. Its narrow streets were pinched between mountain cliffs, false-fronted stores, false-fronted saloons, tents, cabins, bordellos, schools, and even a church.

The local newspaper editor wrote, "It's day all day in the daytime, and there is no night in Creede." Willow Creek ran yellow with stain from mine tailings. Amethyst crystals rattled in schoolchildren's pockets, and the railroad rattled into Creede.

By then, the early 1890s, the Denver and Rio Grande Railroad had had plenty of experience in fitting its rails into tight places in order to tap revenues from the mining country of the Rockies. Narrow-gauge trains that had entered the San Luis Valley by crawling up Muleshoe Curve and over La Veta Pass in the 1870s soon were on their way through Toltec Gorge to reach Durango and the mines near Silverton. A narrow-gauge line also was carved across Poncha Pass into the north end of the Valley to haul ores from Bonanza and from Orient, where iron was shipped to Pueblo's mills. Tracks had spread across the agricultural expanses of the Valley beyond Alamosa to Monte Vista, Del Norte, and even the spa at Wagon Wheel Gap before Creede boomed.

The extension into Creede was to serve the mines for many years. Finally, in recent years, when Creede's mines seemed to sigh a weary if not final gasp, the old rail line faced abandonment.

These historical events were the beginnings of changes that would affect the physical region for years to come. Excursion passengers rode the train to a holiday at Wagon Wheel Gap. Good fishing in the Rio Grande and a mineral spring to soothe aching joints were augmented by hotels and dude ranches. Meanwhile, working ranches around Creede and the upper reaches of the Rio Grande opened their doors to paying guests who enjoyed roughing it out West.

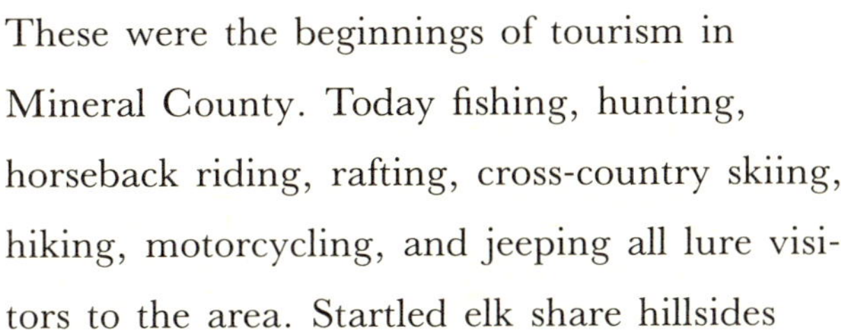

These were the beginnings of tourism in Mineral County. Today fishing, hunting, horseback riding, rafting, cross-country skiing, hiking, motorcycling, and jeeping all lure visitors to the area. Startled elk share hillsides with vacation homes on acres of prime winter range.

With mining an unpredictable source of employment these days, tourism is a welcome boost to the local economy, and Creede itself has become an important drawing card. Shops, restaurants, and old-time saloons attract crowds who rub elbows along the town's narrow streets and drive up the hill to take a snapshot of an old mine's loading chutes or of the local "Boot Hill." Like souvenirs of a bygone era, antiquated buildings remain, and the Creede Repertory Theatre moved into one of them a few years ago. Excellent dramatic productions are complemented by art exhibits, music recitals, poetry readings, and children's theater—more culture than Soapy Smith and Bob Ford knew existed when they were dealing cards and whiskey here almost a century ago.

Modern changes have enriched human life, but the crowds they attract create stresses in the natural environment. People pass through Creede to discover the recreational wonderlands beyond it as persistently as determined prospectors once explored the mountains. Miners left deep wounds on the flanks of the sleeping giant, some of which never have healed. Modern man, slowly, is learning lessons from these scars.

Poncha Pass in the north end of the San Luis Valley is a bridge linking the San Juan and Sangre de Cristo mountain ranges. The latter, the eastern rim of the basin, is a knife edge of peaks running from the Arkansas River on the north all the way to Santa Fe, New Mexico, on the south. These relatively young, jagged mountains contrast in many ways with the San Juans.

The Sangre de Cristos were formed by folding and faulting, causing what geologists call "unconformity" but what laymen call spectacular beauty. Soaring high above timberline, the summits of the Sangre de Cristos often are their most spectacular in evening, when they blush crimson with alpenglow.

A Spanish padre had his own explanation for this phenomenon. The priest, according to legend, was Francisco Torres, accompanying a Spanish expedition to the mountains in search of gold, during the early period of colonization in New Mexico and prior to settlement in the Valley. Perhaps this party was headed to the mysterious mine on Marble Mountain, on the east side of the range, or perhaps they sought treasure in the canyons on Blanca Peak's slopes.

Attacked by their Indian slaves as the expedition entered the mountains, the story goes, the Spaniards retreated to San Luis Lake and sought refuge there on a raft, but the priest had been mortally wounded during the retreat. Looking up at the mountains, glowing red in the twilight, the dying man exclaimed with his last breath, "Sangre de Cristo!" Thus, the range came to be named for the blood of Christ.

Between San Luis Lake and the mountains lies an enormous mass of buff-colored sand, approximately fifty-five square miles of it. The highest dune rises 700 feet. These are the tallest dunes on the North American continent, and not merely because they start at 8,000 feet above sea level at their base.

These towering, undulating sand dunes do not conform to human expectations of mountain scenery, hundreds of miles from any ocean. Still, tourists who have traveled great distances to visit them have been known to ask park rangers, "How do we get to the beach?"

Material making up the dunes is chiefly debris carried by streams to the Valley's floor from the San Juan Mountains. It is theorized that the Rio Grande at one time flowed as far east as San Luis Lake's present site, and the deep bed of deposited sand is consequently much closer to the dunes than is the river's present channel. Prevailing southwesterly winds carried sand toward the pocket now occupied by the dunes, and, as winds lost velocity in their encounter with the mountains, sand was dropped. This process still continues. Winds that sometimes blow from the east help stabilize the dunes, although lower edges of the mass continue to migrate and engulf shrubs and trees in their path.

This sea of sand was set aside as Great Sand Dunes National Monument in 1932, following a campaign instituted by a group of ladies from Monte Vista. Their efforts have been justified as the monument, administered by the National Park Service, attracts thousands of sightseers annually while protecting the natural resource from commercial encroachments.

Aside from tourists, Great Sand Dunes is home to few other living things. Only a few species of creatures with unfamiliar names such as tiger beetle and camel cricket, scurfpea and rice grass can survive on the shifting, often scorching sand. More common are herds of mule deer that populate the monument's surrounding woods and grassland. Still, man with his fertile imagination has bestowed all manner of events on the dunes—disappearing wagon trains and herds of sheep, webbed-footed horses and Indian ambushes. And who is to say what happenings have occurred or not occurred in a place where footprints are erased overnight?

The ruggedness and sheer height of the Sangre de Cristos also inspire a sense of mystery and awe. On these rocky slopes few traces of activity, past or present, exist. True, there are game trails with the tracks of deer, black bear, bighorn sheep, bobcat, mountain lion, and coyote; but, except near fringes of forest merging with grassland, wildlife seems misleadingly to be scarce. Only deer are bold enough to be familiar sights. In the mountains around the Valley, space is deep with hidden habitats, and wildlife need not appear as if on command for viewing. Their activities are governed by their own needs and instincts.

A range like the Sangre de Cristos, because of its inaccessibility, poses more questions than answers for the average observer. Slopes and outcrops of metamorphic rock are rugged, and broad valleys that might permit penetration are rare, the one exception being Sangre de Cristo Creek, leading to La Veta Pass. Consequently, these mountains are a barrier both to travel and to understanding the life that exists in them.

Fragmentary evidence tells that prehistoric peoples occupied temporary camps in the pinyon-juniper woodlands on lower slopes. Were these people gathering nuts and berries and hunting game? Were they on pilgrimages to Blanca Peak, a sacred mountain in Pueblo mythology? Were they collecting ceremonial feathers to carry to their homes to the south? Were they the ones who in a time of hunger scarred ponderosa pine trees to remove a nutritious layer of tissue beneath the bark? Did they cross the high, narrow game trails that later Indians used when traveling in and out of the Valley? Did they pursue mammoths and ancient buffalo through the lower passes? The answers are songs whistled by the wind.

Spanish *conquistadores* left tantalizing scraps of information in reports and journals about their own subsequent travels through this northern frontier of their province, New Mexico. They mentioned searches for mines, skirmishes with Indians, threats of foreign intrusions from the north and east, a little fort on Sangre de Cristo Pass, another across the Valley on San Antonio Mountain.

In the late 1500s Don Juan de Onate is said to have traveled north in the San Luis Valley, where he discovered mines between Culebra and Trinchera creeks. At some time, too, a fort was built to protect these mines. Arrastras, stones on which ore is ground, have been found in a canyon running down from Blanca Peak as well as across the Valley in the mountains near Summitville. These are threads of evidence on which tales of Spanish treasure have been woven.

Because of the hardships experienced in forced labor, including working Spaniards' mines, the natives rebelled, driving the conquerors from the entire territory of New Mexico in the late 1600s and closing up the mine entrances as emphasis. These acts added to the aura of mystery and spawned tales of lost treasure that persist today. Some of the mines never were found or worked again. Perhaps there was a failure of spirit, for it is said that searchers of *tesoros,* treasures, must work together in harmony if they are to succeed.

The Valley still was Spanish territory when the first foreign fur traders ventured across Sangre de Cristo Pass, near La Veta Pass, in the 1700s. This trappers' route was to come as close to a main trail for soldiers and braves as the mountain range offered for the next few decades.

The Valley still was Spanish territory, too, when Zebulon Montgomery Pike and his companions entered it from the Wet Mountain Valley in 1807. Passing the dunes, Pike paused to climb one of the highest, from which he viewed the San Juan Mountains in the distance and the great land between the ranges, and he wrote the first description of it in English. From here the party turned southward and established a camp where the American flag was raised for the first time in the Valley, briefly, for Spanish dragoons soon appeared and arrested Pike.

Less than two decades later the Valley was Mexican territory when American fur trappers began to use the old trail across Sangre de Cristo Pass regularly. In addition to this route to the trading center at Taos, they occasionally crossed Mosca

Pass, on their way to Cochetopa Pass and trading posts in western Colorado and eastern Utah.

American forces had marched into Santa Fe and raised their flag over the governor's palace only fourteen months before Fremont's expedition, with some effort, stumbled onto the right trail across the Sangre de Cristos in November 1848, en route to disaster in the San Juans. For the next half century Americans in many roles were to pursue their manifest destinies arduously across the Sangre de Cristos. Soldiers and prospectors followed traces left by game, Indians, and trappers in the clamor to reap the bounty of a new land, even before the last of the Indians who claimed it as home had been evicted.

By the 1870s a narrow-gauge railroad grade had been forced over La Veta Pass and a wagon road of sorts was hacked down Mosca Pass as the influx of pioneers increased. Some were farmers and ranchers, but the lure of striking it rich with gold and silver continued to draw newcomers and their suppliers of goods across the mountains.

Not finding what they sought elsewhere, some opened and closed short-lived mines on Blanca Peak's shoulders, north in the canyons around Crestone, south in the Culebra Range. But these were not the bonanzas that create boom towns and tycoons. Other than longer lasting iron producers at Orient, east of Villa Grove, and at Russell, at the foot of La Veta Pass, mines in the Sangre de Cristos were flurries leaving prospect holes, wagon roads, and foundations of cabins to become overgrown with quaking aspens and mountain mahogany, nature's more persistent pioneers.

Private landholdings along the base of the Sangre de Cristos gradually fenced off, both literally and figuratively, access to much of the range. In the twentieth century, the mountains have become less rather than better known. After the railroad moved its grade south from La Veta Pass, train passengers glimpsed scenery along its route through the Culebra Range until passenger service ended. At La Veta Pass, highway construction opened a wedge through the mountains for modern auto travel, and this road today offers the sole, common experience of the Sangre de Cristos.

It is true that there are other means of encountering these mountains. Determined and well-equipped jeepers can climb a steep road across Hayden Pass from the north end of the Valley to the Arkansas River Valley. Others thrash their way through sand and water on the Medano Pass Road. Otherwise, foot travel is the means of access.

The most moderate of such treks is in Mosca Pass, with access from Great Sand Dunes National Monument. For hardier adventurers, there are the fourteeners, beckoning mountaineers to add one more peak to their lists.

Nine of Colorado's summits over 14,000 feet high lie in the Sangre de Cristos. Blanca Peak, its massif looming like a sentinel keeping watch over the entire Valley, is the state's fourth highest mountain, and it has three other summits over 14,000 feet for immediate neighbors—Mount Ellingwood, Little Bear, and Lindsey. To the north lies a magnificent cluster comprised of Crestone Peak, Crestone Needle, and Kit Carson Peak, along with its satellite Challenger Peak. To the south Culebra Peak soars above the 14,000-foot mark in the Culebra Range of the Sangre de Cristos. Over in the San Juans, San Luis Peak alone reaches such exhilarating heights, the approaches by road being more problematical than the final hike to the top of this remote fourteener.

The Sangres all demand respect. As a popular hiking guide advises, the climbs are not a problem "so long as visibility is good and the cliffs can be seen and avoided."

The U.S. Weather Bureau reports that the sun shines over the Valley for at least part of almost every day of the year. The Sangre de Cristos, however, have their own climate, which occasionally includes clouds creeping up their east slopes and sagging like wet rags over the summits and in the passes. The San Juans, too, may be blanketed in clouds, flowing in from the southwest, while the Valley itself basks under a blue sky. The mountains are a world apart.

Ruggedness and remoteness have combined to keep large portions of the mountains around the Valley a wilderness. At one time in America's history, wilderness was considered to be a waste of resources, a condition in need of taming and correction. Although part of the Sangre de Cristos has been recommended for designation as wilderness so that scenery, wildlife, and recreational values can be protected in their natural state for future generations, its status has not yet been determined by law.

There is a longing for peace, beauty, and continuity to be found in the mountains and hills surrounding the San Luis Valley. Who is to say that an Indian standing atop Blanca Peak or shaking pinyon nuts and gathering wild currants along the slopes below did not feel the same pleasures and satisfactions that we today experience in those unspoiled places? And who would deny them to people yet unborn?

Descending the long, gentle slope from Poncha Pass into the Valley can be a mystical experience. Nothing written by geographers quite prepares one for the immensity of this moonscape with its mountain ranges on either side and the huge sweep of land between them. Even for those who have traveled the route again and again, the vista takes their breath away. Yet, isolated as it is from other regions by the mountains, the basin presents a sheltered, comfortingly secure aspect when viewed from the north.

For those who have wandered far, the Valley lying ahead seems to murmur, "You are home, safe at last."

From the pass down beyond Villa Grove a little way, the ever-widening neck of the Valley once was called Homan's Park, so named to honor a member of Gunnison's surveying team in the 1850s. The title fell into disuse long ago, sadly, for this high area of grassland and shrub growth deserves a special designation, differing as it does from the rest of the Valley floor. Its elevation drops gradually for about a thousand feet through a transition of vegetation, from pine and fir and aspen groves through scrub oak, sagebrush, and grasses. In winter this section belongs to the mountains with snow piling up in drifts as cold wind whistles down from the pass. In summer, though, cattle and horses share the sun-warmed meadows with deer, pronghorns, and occasionally elk. Long gone are the herds of wild buffalo that once attracted hunters here.

South of Villa Grove grassland gives way to the low scrub that covers much of the Valley floor. Greasewood, also called "chico," survives in areas where drainage is poor and the soil alkaline. The monotony of this drab vegetation is interrupted with patches of rabbitbrush on slightly higher ground. Rabbitbrush festoons large areas of otherwise bleak terrain with golden sprays of flowers in late summer and tawny seed heads that remain all winter. Probably it was this shrub to which Pike referred when he described the Valley in winter as being "a luxuriant vale, crowned with perennial flowers, like a terrestrial paradise, shut out from the view of man."

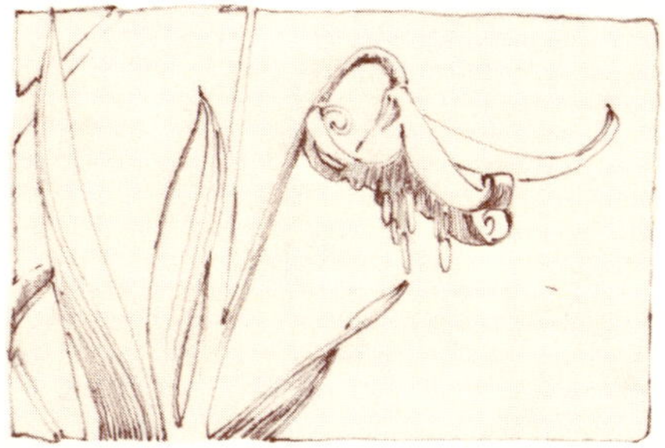

Occasionally the gray carpet of brush gives way to green swaths of marsh, too. Fed by springs, these boggy places are deep with cattails and sedges, alive with ducks, egrets, rails, redwings, marsh wrens, song sparrows, snipe, and many other birds.

Many such oases are springs rising from a confined aquifer that stores drain water beneath layers of clay. This water comes up at fault contacts from deep in the earth. Some of the springs are geothermal with temperatures of about 120 degrees Fahrenheit. The San Luis Valley is Colorado's principal geothermal area, and it includes not only the Valley proper but also the eastern San Juan Mountains and the Rio Grande's drainage basin as far west as Creede and Antelope Warm Springs. Among the best-known sites in this large field are Mineral Hot Springs and Valley View, both being southeast of Villa Grove, Wagon Wheel Gap Hot Springs near Creede, and an area northwest of Blanca. Several wells tapping thermal waters have been used for recreation and for heat.

In addition, thousands of artesian wells have been drilled into the confined aquifer chiefly for agricultural purposes throughout the Valley. More recently additional thousands of other wells have provided water from the unconfined aquifer which is nearer the surface. This resource also is being used for agriculture.

Such abundance of water in an arid region is explained by the location of the Rio Grande Rift and its geology. This cleft extends from New Mexico north to the upper Arkansas Valley near Leadville. The rift is the meeting place of volcanic activity and faults that occurred in the creation of the mountains. The downward thrust of these great faults caused the huge fissure that has been filled with thousands of feet of alluvial debris, washing and blowing down from the mountains. The depression also contains lava flows.

Precipitation in the Valley is scant, only six to ten inches per year, but several streams drain the watershed of the mountains into the basin. In the north end of the Valley many creeks begin bravely enough, only to disappear eventually into the porous, sandy alluvium. San Luis and Kerber creeks, Saguache, Carnero, and La Garita are arteries flowing from the north and northwest. On the east several streams tumble from the steep flanks of the Sangre de Cristos to mingle with other waters in an area that is called the Closed Basin. Medano Creek, a seasonal stream flowing along the southern edge of the sand dunes before disappearing beneath the surface, is a conspicuous example of this phenomenon.

The Closed Basin lies north of the Rio Grande with its lowest point being east of Mosca and Hooper. San Luis and Head lakes, along with a few smaller ponds, occur there, and seep water also may be seen standing in this area where ground water is near the surface. This low point, lacking drainage, is called "the sump."

The great water resource in this portion of the Valley now is being tapped by the federal Closed Basin Project, designed to convey water to the Rio Grande. Purposes of the project are to fulfill interstate compact agreements for water delivery and to benefit Valley water users along the Rio Grande and the Conejos River.

To mitigate the Closed Basin's impact on wetland vegetation and wildlife habitat, water will be diverted also to lands administered by the Bureau of Land Management and by the U.S. Fish and Wildlife Service. As part of the project, also, San Luis Lake and Russell Lakes near Saguache are becoming state wildlife management areas with improvements in their habitats. The effects of all these recent changes will be seen through future generations.

Change is not new in the Closed Basin, however. The most dramatic historical evidence lies in hundreds of acres of alkaline land that once yielded wheat and other crops. Irrigation canals and ditches, many of them abandoned long ago, permitted farming where only grazing had been attempted previously. Towns with grain elevators and mills, banks and hotels emerged on the landscape, and vestiges of some, such as Moffat, Hooper, and Mosca, remain while others disappeared entirely after salts ruined the soil and farms were vacated.

Agricultural development in the Valley began with the first Spanish-speaking settlers, who brought with them more modest but well-adapted techniques for irrigating crops and pastures. Although some of their crops were bartered, these people were intent on sustaining themselves with relatively small farms. More advanced ideas, planting larger fields with cash crops and watering them with canals as big as many a river in the West, came with later English-speaking and European farmers. Land sales, colonization by immigrant groups, town settlement, commercial growth, and networks of rail transportation changed the face of the Valley forever, with towns like Monte Vista, Center, and La Jara becoming major hubs of agricultural activity, for the Valley lived up to the hopes of farmers and ranchers where land lies higher than in the sump.

Alfalfa, vegetables, potatoes, and barley became the backbone of the Valley's economy. Today potatoes and barley usually are alternated in successive years. Storage and shipping facilities also play a vital role in the region's life.

Ranching also began with the early Hispanic settlers, who brought flocks of sheep, some cattle, and hogs with them when they came up the Rio Grande from their former homes in New Mexico to settle land grants around San Luis and Conejos. A few sheep owners, particularly in the neighborhoods of Ortiz and Del Norte, would amass huge flocks in time.

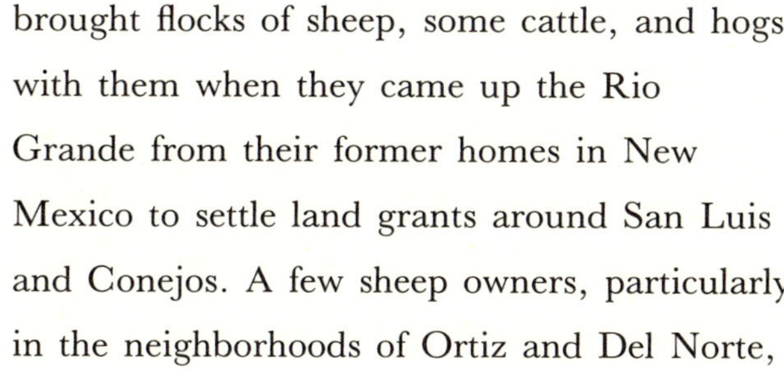

Larger herds of cattle arrived from Texas and from the east with English-speaking owners. Both sheep and cattle holdings increased until the normal patterns of summer grazing in the mountains and winter feeding in the Valley caused overuse, and range wars similar to those elsewhere in the West erupted. Violence was not uncommon in the Valley, especially along the base of the Sangre de Cristos from

Blanca Peak northward, where great numbers of animals grazed. The long arm of the law could not reach far enough from existing county seats, as fences were cut, homes burned, and livestock killed or stolen.

A century ago annual migrations of livestock also turned the San Juans into scenes of violence and bloodshed. In a partly successful effort to resolve the antagonism between sheepmen and cattlemen, citizens attempted to separate animals and their caretakers along arbitrary, physical boundaries. Different streams marked off different parts of the watershed as pasturage for sheep or for cattle. Even different streets in the town of Del Norte were assigned to sheep or cattle being driven to the railroad.

Ultimately the range wars resulted in the creation of federal agencies that now are a familiar part of life in the region. Around the turn of the century, with enmity between livestockmen still raging, the federal government stepped in and established timber reserves. These reserves were designed primarily to protect natural resources, such as forest and minerals, but they also enabled control of the public lands that were being used by sheep and cattle owners. In 1907 the original forest reserves became national forests, one of these being Rio Grande National Forest, which takes in most of the mountains surrounding the San Luis Valley. Since the 1940s the Bureau of Land Management has administered grazing districts on other federal public lands.

One of the large ranches on private land occupies what began as a land grant, the Baca No. 4. This never was a typical grant like those doled out by Spanish and Mexican governments. Rather, it was given after the San Luis Valley had passed from Mexican possession into United States territory. In the 1860s the United States gave the Baca Grant in exchange for another parcel of land to the heirs of the original donee, Luis Maria de Baca. It quickly passed into other hands, beginning with its purchase by Colorado's first territorial governor, William Gilpin, and followed by a rancher who established a large herd of purebred cattle there.

The Baca also was the scene of mining activity that drew hundreds of prospectors and squatters. The railroad extended a line onto the grant during this excitement. The squatters were evicted, leaving a scattering of ghost towns along the edge of the mountains as they went. In recent years the property has been the site of a working ranch, a tranquil mountain-home development complete with a golf course, conference centers, and an enormous blank spot on maps where the land grant lies.

Readers of maps will find another blank space on some maps, east of the Rio Grande in the southern portion of the Valley. Whereas most mountainous areas around the Valley fall into the Rio Grande National Forest and are duly mapped, the Culebra Range is in private hands, primarily those of publisher Malcolm Forbes. How such a vast piece of prime real estate should be privately owned is another story linked to a land grant, the Sangre de Cristo.

This Mexican grant, like others elsewhere, gave a huge parcel to individuals who, in turn, were expected to encourage colonization there. The Sangre de Cristo Grant included all of the land in the Valley lying east of the Rio Grande to the crest of the Culebras and north to Blanca Peak. At the time the grant was made, in the 1840s, the San Luis Valley still was occupied by nomadic Indians, who, though primitive, had acquired horses long since and were both mobile and troublesome. Their frequent excursions into the Valley were largely responsible for the grant's not becoming settled for a few years. When the first colonists did arrive, Indians rode off with livestock and grain and left murdered victims behind them. Occasionally, instead of stealing goods, Utes traded Navajo Apache hostages, or Navajos traded Utes, and these native people were assimilated into family life as servants. It was a harsh land with stern living conditions which only the hardiest settlers survived.

With oxen, horses, and burros they came, nevertheless, from the villages of northern New Mexico, where arable land and good pasture were scarce. With them, too, came sheep and goats, pigs and chickens, corn and beans and wheat to plant. In the hard earth they dug the ditches that carried water from Culebra and Costilla creeks to their farms near the first communities. These first villages were near today's Costilla, now part of New Mexico, and San Luis. Their water rights along the Culebra would be the first recorded in Colorado Territory a few years later.

Passing from a Mexican possession, the Valley became part of New Mexico Territory, a possession of the United States after the Mexican War. With this change came protection by the army at posts, such as Fort Massachusetts at the foot of Blanca Peak and its replacement, Fort Garland. These installations encouraged increased settlement.

Even with military protection, newcomers preferred to live in compact, adobe villages, drawn together around a plaza for mutual defense and to venture out to the fields only during the day. Remnants of old adobe towns and farms still can be seen in Costilla and Conejos counties, as well as near Del Norte in Rio Grande County.

It was a pastoral life with farming, hunting, and sheepraising sustaining the people. Men and women, boys and girls, young and old worked to till the earth and irrigate crops, to grind corn, to gather firewood from the nearby mountains, to shear wool and weave blankets and garments from it, to heal the body with native herbs and the soul with faith, to amuse themselves with homemade toys, games, dances, and horse races.

This isolated life, demanding self-reliance and steadfast cooperation at the same time, was slow to change. After statehood came to Colorado, with cultural changes in the Valley occurring at accelerating rates, the Hispanic people retained many of their conservative patterns of life. English-speaking newcomers, European colonizers, Oriental farmers all were the foreigners in areas where Spanish remained the dominant language. For a long time, even that language remained the archaic Castilian Spanish spoken by the *conquistadores*.

This traditional culture was strongest in the southern part of Costilla County, where lands of the old Sangre de Cristo Grant remained largely in the hands of Hispanic families. The northern part of the grant changed hands after land developers divided the property into the Costilla and the Trinchera estates. In the Trinchera portion a large ranch was acquired and passed through the ownership of various wealthy families before it became the Forbes Trinchera, more properly known as Sangre de Cristo Ranches, Inc., a mountain subdivision.

On the west side of the Rio Grande in Conejos County, patterns of settlement and culture were similar to those in Costilla County for the first few years. Hispanics arrived to establish homes on a land grant, but the United States Congress declared it to be invalid in the 1860s. As a result, Conejos County was opened to homesteading. A mixture of several cultural groups developed in consequence, and the lives of Spanish-speaking settlers were subjected to change. However, whether people of Conejos County attended Catholic, Mormon, Dunkard, Presbyterian, or Methodist church services, they shared two common needs—land and water. Irrigation ditches came from the Conejos River, La Jara Creek, the Alamosa River, and Rock Creek, and the value of land was tied to the value of the water rights.

Transportation further differentiated life in the two counties. Originally the principal routes in the Valley had been two wagon roads leading to and from the settlements of northern New Mexico. Travelers rattled along one or the other with the Rio Grande effectively determining not only the choice of roads but one's markets, schools, churches, and neighbors as well. In time a few small bridges spanned the Rio Grande, but life on either side of the river still remained physically separate.

The river was no match for one challenger, the railroad. After crossing the Sangre de Cristos and passing through northern Costilla County, the tracks of the Denver and Rio Grande spanned the river at its big bend, the site of today's Alamosa. This location would become a division point and a commercial center for the Valley. With the birth of Adams State College, the community also became the educational center for the entire region some years later.

The arrival of the railroad soon had a dramatic impact on life in Conejos County, for tracks quickly were laid south to Antonito and then west over Cumbres Pass to reach the mining country across the San Juans. South of Antonito, the

"Chili Line" continued into New Mexico to serve traffic there. Just as crops thrived wherever ribbons of ditch water ran, so towns thrived wherever ribbons of railroad track ran.

Like a magnet the railroad drew workers, merchants, and goods to be shipped. Produce, livestock, wool, ore, timber, and ties arrived at loading docks to be shipped out of the Valley. Smoke from narrow-gauge locomotives smudged the air, tracing, miles away, the route of the clickety-clicking wheels. Along the grade ducks and geese scattered, a deer twitched its ears and bounded away through a meadow, a farm wife gathering wild asparagus looked up and waved at the engineer, and then it was gone.

Silence. For large segments of the Valley's population, the silence was deafening when trackage was abandoned in modern times, as trucks took over a large share of the freighting business and passenger traffic was discontinued entirely.

Although narrow-gauge trains now carry tourists through Toltec Gorge and over Cumbres Pass in summer, silence lies on the tracks in the long winter months. Daily freights, pulled by diesel engines, rumble through the Valley, but silence lies on their tracks, too, for hour on end. Locomotive whistles are almost, but not quite, forgotten.

Silence. Along rural roads the silence can seem as deep as the sky over the Valley, but, listening to it, one begins to hear mysterious noises—blackbirds rasping somewhere in the cattails, geese honking overhead, a chirp, a twitter, a rattle, a hoot, a chorus of guroos, tuk-tuks, and onks. The silence is filled with a cacophony of sound. The silence is especially noisy in a wildlife refuge, where thousands of migrating and nesting birds contribute to the din in the Valley. The U.S. Fish and Wildlife Service manages two refuges near Alamosa and Monte Vista, while the state maintains other areas.

Each spring and autumn witness processions of birds traveling through the Valley along the course traced by the Rio Grande. It is a migration route through the Rocky Mountains that has been used for millions of years. When modern changes on the continent threatened the survival of birds everywhere, the Valley's refuges were established as part of a network of lands set aside to protect them.

Like some other wildlife refuges throughout the nation, the Alamosa-Monte Vista complex permits specified human activities on its lands. Points of access are limited to foot travel on the Alamosa Refuge, but the Avocet Trail Tour Route offers opportunities to visit a large portion of the Monte Vista Refuge. Visitors come for birdwatching, photography, outdoor education, and even hunting. Hunting may seem contrary to the goals of a wildlife refuge, but this sport is justified by the fact that hunters have helped acquire lands for refuges. These sportsmen must purchase Federal Migratory Bird Hunting and Conservation Stamps, popularly called "duck stamps," and all revenues from their sale are used for the acquisition of refuge land.

Waterfowl find such suitable habitat on these refuges that breeding populations have increased greatly, reversing trends that appeared to spell doom a generation ago. The nationwide pattern is exemplified at the Valley's refuges, where thousands of ducks and geese enjoy ponds and moist grasslands. Shorebirds such as avocets, phalaropes, and terns are joined by ibis, egrets, herons, and countless other species.

Considering the vast amount of acreage bristling with nests, to say nothing of rodents and other creatures great and small, it is not surprising that predators also make the refuges their homes. Among these uninvited animals are coyotes, badgers, skunks, and raccoons, usually well-hidden by vegetation. In contrast, birds of prey are conspicuous, whether on the wing or perched on a utility pole, and observers quickly discover how many raptors exist not only at the refuges but also throughout the Valley.

Four-legged predators generally are unpopular with ranchers, who tally the loss of lambs and calves in terms of dollars and cents. Raptors, on the other hand, can be beneficial as they help control populations of rabbits, mice, and other rodents.

The Valley has large numbers of hawks in summer and winter, while a common sight is a northern harrier sweeping the fields in search of a meal or a kestrel sitting on a power line awaiting lunch. Falcons are fairly common, and rare peregrines occasionally descend from their canyon homes to hunt in the Valley. Joining native birds are peregrine falcons placed in the rocky cliffs of Conejos Canyon as part of a program to reestablish these endangered birds.

Owls—great horned, short-eared, long-eared, burrowing, pygmy, flammulated, saw-whet, and boreal—go about their rounds grabbing a midnight snack. Golden eagles, a thrill for visitors, are almost too numerous to be noteworthy among local residents.

Noteworthy, though, are bald eagles. Endangered in status and thrilling to watch, they are among the spectacles that always seem to elicit a gasp of admiration from viewers. With breeding grounds and winter habitat reduced, populations dropped until they were protected. In winter, when temperatures plummet, the bald eagles arrive from the north to spend a few months. By day they fish any open water they can find in the rivers or snatch ducks from fields when ice prevents fishing. In the evening, their day's feeding completed, they congregate in groves of trees that are roosts habitually used by different flocks. As many as fifty or sixty eagles may roost together, soaring on huge wings that span six or seven feet, to join their companions at sundown.

No shrinking violets when it comes to size are the sandhill cranes that migrate through the Valley in spring and fall. Standing about four feet tall, they have wings measuring six to seven feet. Thousands of cranes fly into the Valley in large flocks, in wave after wave. They settle in meadows and in fields of barley stubble, where they eat fallen grain. Resting in isolated areas, they may be unseen, but they can be heard at great distances as their constant chatter fills the air, one of the memorable sounds of the Valley.

The San Luis Valley is a migration stopover for the cranes. The birds nest in Idaho and northeastern Utah and winter in New Mexico and Mexico. Their stay in the Valley lasts for six to eight weeks, and in spring courtship displays and dancing are added to the activities of resting and eating.

Inevitably, some farmers resent these large, uninvited guests, especially when they arrive in fields after sowing or before harvest, but for the most part the coming of the cranes overrides ordinary human priorities. There is an assurance in the seasonal movement, in the haunting *garoo-a* that fills the Valley, in gray clouds of birds winging their way against a red sunset. The cranes seem to say that life on the planet continues, with or without man's interference, season after season, pretty much as it should be.

When the cranes arrive from the south as early as February, the last bald eagles have not yet departed for Montana and Canada. And when the last cranes moving south linger as late as December, some bald eagles may have arrived. This overlapping in migration may permit wildlife enthusiasts the rare opportunity of seeing bald eagles and whooping cranes on the same day.

Traveling with the thousands of sandhill cranes have been a handful of whoopers. The largest birds on the North American continent, standing five feet tall, whooping cranes have become the symbol of the conservation movement. Numbering only sixteen in the wild in 1950, this species, hopefully, is being saved from the brink of extinction by means of a variety of repopulation efforts. One unique scheme has been the removal of whooping crane eggs from selected nests in Canada for incubation by sandhill cranes in Idaho at Gray's Lake National Wildlife Refuge. This strategy is based on observations that whooping cranes usually have not succeeded in hatching and rearing both of their two offspring. Also, foster parents among the sandhills were chosen on the basis of their own successful traits in incubating and raising their young.

After being hatched by their adoptive parents, whoopers migrated with sandhills on a comparatively short flyway to the Bosque del Apache Refuge in New Mexico, a migration that was hoped to be less hazardous than the long route from Canada to the Gulf Coast, the normal flyway of whooping cranes. En route between Idaho and New Mexico, the adopted whoopers could rest and feed in the San Luis Valley with the sandhill cranes.

This program, designed to augment the whooping crane population, did not fulfill its primary purpose, although as many as twenty-seven whoopers were seen migrating in the Valley one year. Fatalities and failure to breed defeated the project, while nationwide numbers increased.

The rarity of the birds, coupled with the tension that surrounds any gamble, has lent the birds a special aura. It is not uncommon to see buses from Denver, St. Louis, or Cincinnati filled with birdwatchers hoping for a glimpse of a whooping crane among the sandhills. In spring Monte Vista's boosters have organized an annual Whooping Crane Festival with tours, lectures, and other activities to educate the public about North America's endangered whooping cranes and the Valley's stake in their survival.

This interest reaches beyond mere commercialization, for local residents feel a sincere curiosity and proud proprietorship regarding these magnificent birds. It is no small responsibility to share a neighborhood with a whooping crane. There was disappointment when the Fish and Wildlife Service announced termination of its project; yet, it had achieved a success in increasing public awareness about endangered wildlife.

Perhaps the whooping cranes have become a symbol not only of the need for conservation but also of hope. The cranes seem to promise that if they can survive, the human race just might make it, too. In a place like the San Luis Valley, people know nature firsthand, and they know they cannot play with nature and survive.

And so it is that people in the Valley listen for the first flock of cranes moving north in early spring. There is assurance in the fact that they made it through the winter. In fall, sounds of the southward-bound birds close the summer. There is a sense of success in that another breeding and growing season has taken place, but there is dread, too. Will the birds survive the months ahead, and will we? Most do.

South they fly, following the ribbon of the river, down the Valley past hazy hills of lava, over the sweeping plains of yucca and sagebrush, past San Antonio Mountain, that great round sentinel guarding the Valley's southern gates. Following the Rio Grande, the river of the north, from its headwaters to strange lands, to other places in other times, the birds go. They represent both the continuity and the never-ending change of the Valley.

GREATER SANDHILL CRANE IN FLIGHT One of the oldest bird species inhabiting the North American continent, the sandhill crane seasonally graces the San Luis Valley with its presence. Seven-foot wingspans and haunting calls of the flock of 22,000 add a special quality to spring and fall.

FALL COTTONWOODS AT DUNES Cottonwood foliage is nurtured by the intermittent flow of Medano Creek at Great Sand Dunes National Monument. The creek succeeds in separating the dunes on one side from growing vegetation on the other.

OVERVIEW OF DUNES AT SUNRISE Wind has deposited and sculpted sand into 700-foot-high dunes at the base of the Sangre de Cristo Range. For a brief period at sunrise the sensuous shapes are fully revealed, to be lost as the sun moves higher in the sky.

AMERICAN BITTERN Usually elusive and difficult to see, this American bittern photographed at the Monte Vista Wildlife Refuge reveals itself to the patient observer. Spending additional time in some of the Valley's numerous unique areas invariably leads to rewarding discoveries.

CRESCENT-SHAPED DUNE A close-up study of a barchan illustrates interplay of light and shadow, subtlety of shape and texture.

ASPEN LEAVES IN STREAM Visible from the main highways but rarely explored, small streams plunge from the Sangre de Cristos. In fall they provide a special beauty, carrying colorful aspen leaves to the valley floor.

DEER TRACKS AND COTTONWOOD LEAVES Mule deer traveling across sandy areas near the dunes leave indistinct tracks. Here, blowing leaves from narrow-leaf cottonwoods have filled in the imprints before the sand has hidden them from our eyes.

DEER AT DUNES Protected from hunting by the national monument's jurisdiction, mule deer thrive within the boundaries. Though they rarely venture into the dunes, deer are readily found in the rabbitbrush and muley grass nearby.

CONEJOS RIVER NEAR PIKE'S STOCKADE The centralized location, open water, and wild game were reasons Zebulon Pike chose this area along the Conejos River for his camp in the winter of 1807. It continues to be prime habitat for wildlife.

LA GARITA ARCH Extensive volcanic activity marked the Valley's west side approximately 18 million years ago. Fissures emanating from one of the volcanoes formed thin dikes or walls. Erosion and weathering have created La Garita Arch.

HELLGATE Slow cooling of basalt formed the distinctive columnar structure seen in Hellgate at the base of Carnero Canyon.

RIDGE BELOW BRISTOL HEAD Shafts of late afternoon light sometimes expose dramatic areas otherwise overlooked, as in this ridge beneath the prominence of Bristol Head, located above the Rio Grande west of Creede.

BLACKBIRD CALLING IN MORNING A harbinger of warmer days ahead when the Valley will abound with song, this redwing blackbird sings in the cold of spring. His frosty breath gives a visual interpretation of the melody.

WILD CHERRY CREEK Both early Spanish and later prospectors searched the mountains surrounding the Valley for gold. Some was actually found in Wild Cherry Canyon and is still to be found in the brilliantly colored autumn leaves.

FOG LIFTING OVER ALAMOSA REFUGE Climatic characteristics of the Valley often result in wide temperature variances. In the lower areas along the Rio Grande, ground fog is common.

WETLAND POND AT ALAMOSA REFUGE The Monte Vista–Alamosa National Wildlife Refuge provides critical habitat for nesting waterfowl and associated species, as well as enjoyment for birdwatchers and sport for hunters. The double-crested cormorants overlooking this pond are just one of the species protected by the refuge.

COLUMBINES AT SCHINZEL FLATS Colorado's state flower, the blue columbine, motivated A. J. Flynn to write "Where the Columbines Grow," which later became the state song. Flynn's inspiration came from seeing carpets of the flowers at Schinzel Flats in the San Juan Mountains below South Fork.

CONEJOS CANYON PATCHWORK IN GREEN Emerald-colored aspen are interrupted by dark, evergreen spikes in this view across the Upper Conejos River. Imagine the colors to be seen in fall when the aspen turn to gold and red.

ASPEN AT SAND DUNES This is a valley of wonders, some hidden from the casual observer. By standing at the visitor center of Great Sand Dunes and looking away from the dunes, one can see exquisite groves of aspen and cottonwoods.

NORTH CLEAR CREEK FALLS The falls on North Clear Creek just above the Rio Grande west of Creede are yet another example of the natural wonders to be found in the San Luis Valley.

ASPEN TREES AND GOLDEN BANNER The yellow blossoms of golden banner (*Thermopis montana*) beneath newly leafed aspen are a sure sign that summer is on the way in the lower reaches of the Conejos River.

CLARET CUP CACTUS At lower elevations brilliant red claret cups (*Echinocereus triglochidiatus*) bloom on rocky slopes and in pinyon-juniper woodlands, providing a refreshing splash of color.

BISON AND CRESTONES Humans have lived in the Valley for approximately 12,000 years. Early hunters came in pursuit of bison. This animal, part of the stock owned by a local rancher, brings back visions of the massive herds once roaming the San Luis Valley.

MOONRISE OVER THE CRESTONES Crestone Needle and Crestone Peak are just two of the nine peaks over 14,000 feet visible from the Valley. Like jewels in a tiara they provide a startling contrast to the flat Valley floor.

ASPEN LEADING INTO THE VALLEY Most of the water descending from the high mountains surrounding the San Luis Valley quickly sinks into the porous valley floor. Vegetation is a graphic indicator of available water, and the quick transition shown here illustrates how rapidly the water is lost.

SNOWY RIDGE BELOW KIT CARSON PEAK Pinnacled ridges beneath lofty summits capture snow the summer sun will turn to water. Porous material composing the Valley floor will absorb most of the runoff within a mile of the mountains.

SANDHILL CRANES IN PRE-DAWN The bitter cold of February greets early migrating sandhill cranes. Before the sun's warming rays can reach them, the cranes remain on their night roost, huddled against the cold.

TWO WHOOPING CRANES CALLING WITH SANDHILLS Part of a foster-parented whooping crane population, these endangered birds have traveled through the San Luis Valley with 22,000 greater sandhill cranes. The two above were known by their colored leg bands as 78-1 and 83-3, designations reflecting the year each whooper egg hatched.

TWO BALD EAGLES IN TREE The Valley is the winter home for several hundred bald eagles migrating from the Arctic North. They sometimes congregate on preferred perches that provide good vantage points to their feeding areas and surroundings.

DUCKS LEAVING WATER AT MONTE VISTA REFUGE

Wetlands, created by river meanders and springs, provide habitat for countless birds. The San Luis Valley is on a major flyway that brings thousands of migrating birds through the area each spring and autumn.

DEADMAN CREEK WITH CLOUD TAPESTRY Trees trace the path of Deadman Creek as it reaches into the Valley with its life-giving water. The vastness of the Valley floor complements the expanse of dramatic skies and clouds.

LILY POND ABOVE PLATORO Although pondlilies are not common in the San Juan Mountains, they occasionally may be found in beaver ponds in spruce and fir forests. These yellow pondlilies (*Nuphar luteum*) are blooming near Stunner Pass.

EXPLODING CUMULUS AND TREE Clear summer skies can create dramatic thermal currents. Along with moisture, these currents often generate swelling cumulus clouds with occasionally brief but intense storms.

WHEELER Aloof and alone in the remote San Juan Mountains near Halfmoon Pass, Wheeler Geologic Area is hidden from the view of all but the most persistent travelers. A highly eroded area of volcanic tuff provides unworldly panoramas.

WHEELER Wind, water, freezing, and thawing have all combined to shape rock into a myriad of towers, sinuous gullies, and pedestaled monuments.

WHEELER The volcanic ash welded by heat into tuff, as seen exposed here, is evidence of the area's violent geological past.

ELEPHANT ROCKS The large shapely boulders found at the west edge of the Valley floor, along with other volcanic remnants, provide a clue to this area's geologic history. Vegetation struggles to gain footholds in the hard environment.

BLANCA PEAK AND RIO GRANDE Water flowing into the San Luis Valley ultimately joins the mighty Rio Grande for its 1800-mile journey to the Gulf of Mexico. The volcanic hills west of San Luis and the massif of Blanca Peak illustrate the diversity of this section of the Valley.